bursting

at the

seams

bursting at the seams

a collection of poetry by Chantel Massey

Published by VK Press, LLC

VK Press, LLC
PO BOX 78044
Indianapolis, IN 46278
www.vkpresses.com

Bursting at the Seams: A Collection of Poetry

www.ChantelMassey.com

Editor: Michael Baumann
Copyeditor: Randie Chapman
Cover Design: Rae Parker
Interior Design: Michael Baumann

First edition published December 2017 in the United States by VK Press, LLC

ISBN 13: 978-0-9982754-3-7 (ebk)
ISBN 13: 978-0-9982754-4-4 (pbk)

dedication

This book was written for all the women in my family: Mamas, sisters, friends (who I also call sisters), Aunties, and cousins.

I love y'all.

contents

"Men have had God for so long but I think it is time for us to have God. I am ready for God to look like me."

—Randie Chapman

acknowledgements

First, I must say glory to God.

Mama I write this for you: I have watched you and learned from you, and I paid close attention to the lessons you've taught, and I believe you to be the most gorgeous woman I have ever known. Your confidence and free spirit are so riveting to me. I hope that is genetic. You are funny and fierce and fire at its bluest and I cannot be more grateful to have you as my mother.

Cousins and my Aunties, I write this for you. My sisters, I write this for you.

My family is amazing; thank you for all your support in anything I do, and thank you for believing in me more than I believed in myself most days. I want to say thank you to all my friends who helped along the way. Manon for telling me I must keep writing, Jessica for telling me to follow my heart, Pope Adrian Bless for asking me for years when I was going to write a book, Randie for pushing me; thank you Everett, my love, for pushing me and so many others who were so supportive throughout this whole process. I cannot thank you enough.

introduction

It was a Sunday when I revamped my website. I sent a
text out to the closest people to me with a link to the
website to see what they thought. Mostly to get their
approval and validation. And they gave it to me as
expected. However—

my mother never replied to the text. Then at work the
next day, I received an email from her entitled
"correction" and read, "All looks good other than the
request below. Have a great day! Love you much
mom" and below was the correction: she wanted me
to make a space between a period and a letter.
Attached was her work information.

In that moment, I desired a deeper relationship with
my mother, one that she felt allowed her to celebrate
with me and be proud of me in any space with me.
Then I thought back to the question of why I needed
to write this book of poetry.

I needed to write because I needed to heal. I needed to
tell myself "I see you, and I am not ashamed of what I
see, and I offer you the same grace I offer everyone
else." I needed to write it because as I learn about
womanhood (as I understand it to be), I've realized

that my understanding has always been controlled for me by others' rules. And my lessons have proved those rules do not protect me, but they in fact hinder me. Hell, they kept me away from my mother and sometimes the deepest and darkest parts of myself that I have been ashamed of. Not knowing that was where the best parts of me were hidden.

These conventional methods of woman and love had to be questioned for my own sanity. I have questioned rape culture effects on family, fighting illness, gossip, sexuality, being in love, falling out of love, healing, womanhood, identity, spirituality, religion, blackness and what it means to be black and/or safe in America as a woman of color.

Still I have found no answer, but just the inspiration, and I share with others how to resist this bullshit the best way I can.

part I. The meeting and the making

"But the picking out, the choosing. Don't ever think I fell for you, or fell over you. I didn't fall in love, I rose in it. I saw you and made up my mind. My mind."

—Toni Morrison, *Jazz*

Popsicles

I understand that you two, split
like wild eyelashes
That her telling you there's someone else
hurt like painful backlashes
I want to help you get rid of those painful memories causing
whiplashes

By loving you

Let me conceive new memories for you
I want to love you the same way second graders love sitting
on a curb
Eating popsicles after chasing an ice cream truck
in the middle of summer

All I ask is that you
allow me to be
the blue ice to
fall against your tongue
and cool you off
with the sweetest "I love you"
Your taste buds have ever known
Come leave your foot prints on the life line of my open
palm
With a collected recollection
Of your cherry Carmex
Swimming in an ocean
Of kisses with my lip gloss
I want to love you the same way Angela Davis loved the
revolution
Our love, it'll be a revolution

I want to love you
the same way Sonia Sanchez

loves repetition
Loves repetition
Loves repetition

Our love will be a repetitive
revolution between humans

So, clear those dust particles
off your aorta and let blood flow
Like diamonds in the fingers
of a jewelry store clerk
because I want to marvel at your beauty

And love you for it,

The same way she forgot to.

9-21-12

At 830am
I cannot help but pretend to sleep
So that you can stretch your fingers
Through my hair like tree branches
And caress my face
Like Communion on Sunday

One last time, I will visit the church home
That I have found in your open palm

Praise the deep brown of your hands
And admire
How they move
When the fire
Flickers off
The tip of your tongue
When you talk
About
Anime

I will let that flame
Lick my imagination with
Its greatness in detail
And elevated tone
That Awakens
The sometimes quiet
pulse in my chest

One last time I want you to revive me.
So,
I could frolic between the sheets of your heart
Like an insomniac

Lay with me like you used to

Head to breast
Hand to hip
My legs wrapped between yours
Like chocolate Twizzlers

Trying to connect the
Same way Ohio fits into the corners
Of Indiana

This was supposed to be the last time

The last time our lips
Danced under covers
Your covers.

Where the shaft of your thumb can own
The back of my ear
On a Sunday morning
And make it hard for me to leave,
Once again.

part II. The transition the outgrowing

"Everything will change. The only question is growing up or decaying."

—Nikki Giovanni

"Your silence will not protect you."

—Audre Lorde

Day One of Molting

"No one will have to know," he said.
Sunday. 9am. Summer break.
No one else around.
My mind doing the runaround.
His arm clasp to my throat
Like a button to a business shirt

Hard to breathe
Tight grip
Prayer to the lip
Legs dancing
prancing or
that was what I imagined

Protector and predator
in the same body
Up against my body.

Small. Twelve. Frail
Fraying to his touch
Wanting to get away

That year I was a broken music box
Dancing backwards
With old jewels and
no rules
on how to value myself so I found a boy.
I could be lost with
And we could wander together.
Playing victim. There was no victor.
Didn't know how to be.

"No one will have to know," rang in my head
So loud and cracked like broken glass.
Angry. Sad. Untrusting. Always fussing.
No new friends.
For years,
this played over and over
But then it dawned on me after seven therapy sessions,
countless sleepless nights
and countless shots

As I stumbled down Ohio streets
I stumbled on my "I can" moment.
I can validate myself.
I can give me what I need.
I can change.
I can be better.

I decided to break the music box
build something better with the rubble
I realized I wasn't boxed
but I was all the music
so

I just let myself play.

Admitting the addiction

I've
begged for love
Bent backwards for love
And forwards for love
To look in my direction
Or call me back

I've
been shameful for love
Anything they wanted me to be for love
A Chameleon
A Pandora's box
A magician for love

To be held, forgiven, wanted

I've
been balled up
Curled at the knees for love
I've called a numerous amount
of times for love
Hoping love would call back

I've
prayed for love
Fasted for love
I've been a fool for love
I've pleaded guilty for love
Even if it was lies

I've
lied for love

Been sad for days for love
Woke up and made breakfast
And even wrote this poem for love
I've been to the dark side
And back for love
Forgave and gave
Again for love
For the love

Not my own

Not God's

And that's where I went wrong.

7-19-16

The flesh on her hips and shoulders
Raw
A blister on her foot
Belly swollen with instinct
Made her a new identity
She got out of the car
Started to walk home
It was only a few miles away
Arm pits musky
Sweat drips from her face to her clavicle
She remembered
How her mama
Would say, "Don't shrink yourself for no man."
Her thoughts went back to the moment
Before she got out of the car
He was yelling
She wanted to remain calm
Not shatter his ego
But failed
Car stopped
He said, "Get out. You can walk home."
There was no hesitation
On her end
No doubt
Only relief
For she had followed her mother's advice
Believed she made her proud
She stood up for herself
Decided single was better than this
Decided it was better to walk home
Than to be treated like this
She was as certain about this decision

As the sky was about who it was.
She faced that fear of lonely
With certainty
Laughter now
One-mile left
18. no children
Just got off work
She is exhausted
And knows that
She birthed confidence
Swarmed with bees
She is sweet
Honey suckled
And fills the sky
She left it full
Night and day
July made her a new identity
One that involved
No mother
No man
A 3-mile walk
And lots of laughter.

Drunken nights

Voices get quiet
Faces get blurry

Under closed eyelids

I search for a vivid memory of you
Here
With me

Where we danced under damp clothes

Beads of condensation bounce off speakers

Your feet try to keep up with my feet
My hands try to keep up with your hands
And the way they trace my body to music.

Your forehead
Rested on
The back of my neck

Your hair sweaty
Half on
The nape of your neck

Half in my hand

My elbow rest on the side of your face

Pelvis to back

We danced

I remember my drunken nights were when
I forgot you were a woman
I forgot about social constructions
And how much they confined us
I forgot about your past and
How you became a martyr for it—

After too many shots I forgot
you did shit like that.

Repeat at least twice a month

By Tuesday,
I forgot how easy it was
To fall asleep without you

Monday,
To fall asleep without you
I had put
The pillow you slept on
Under my face

Sunday,
I fell asleep without you
After I pushed all the pillows
Up against my body and
Found the one that smelled like you

Each time
I slept

I missed you

Even if I didn't want to.

part III. The Gossip

"If I didn't define myself for myself, I would be crunched into other people's fantasies for me and eaten alive."

—Audre Lorde

They Say

This is generational
In the 1960s
Girls become the Talk at Christmas
Parties when they don't want to
Participate

Because of that *thing* that happened.
Word gets out.
It takes Mama 5 days to ask Aunt for help.
Aunt helps and it takes 5 minutes for her to chat,
Thinks she is helping
Because of that *thing* that happened.

In the 1980s
Girls become the Talk at Christmas
Parties when their dresses
are too tight
Because of that *thing* that happened.
Word gets out.
It takes Mama 5 days to ask Aunt for help.
Aunt helps and it takes 5 minutes for her to chat,
Thinks she is helping
Because of that *thing* that happened.

In the 2010s
Girls become the Talk at Christmas
Parties when they don't want to
Participate in this year's
Family activities
Because of that *thing* that happened.
Word gets out.
It takes Mama 5 days to ask Aunt for help.
Aunt helps and it takes 5 minutes for her to chat,
Thinks she is helping
Because of that *thing* that happened.

Daughters stand bone stiff in the Talk

Rumors boil to the surface—a rash
Itchy, dry,
Leaving daughters bristling with embarrassment about
The stories we tell   or don't
The shame we feel   or don't
Beware: We've all been the Talk—sex, rape, molestation
Beware: And we've all turned other girls into Talk at
Christmas
Parties too

Beware: of the stories they tell   or don't   that will come
back again.

Ode to Sula

She be the one they gossip about
Got everything to say about
But don't understand
No wonder they all keep coming back
They want to crawl between her parted legs and rest
Make themselves at home
But they did not know
That she robbed men who found joy in her smile
And God on her inner thighs
Longing to be baptized by the wetness of her tongue
With praises of "Damn Daddy, do it just like that."
She would straddle the hips of their hearts
Collecting warm throbbing pulses to revive her own

Woman

She was no ordinary woman
She was her *own*
Woman
She hid well
Behind burning brass eyes
that didn't sit too far from her forehead
Complimenting her narrow face when she smiled
With confidence
standing on long bandy legs
that men thought cried for their attention
They thought they cried for their attention

They wanted to rub their feet in her hair
Be her savior
Play her husband

But she had no interest in becoming wife
What she believed to be a
Woman
In
Frivolous
Eternal
Bondage:

The state of being bound to or subjected by some external force
No,
She enjoyed the power she got
From men who craved
Her and women who hated her
From threatening their Christian households
They couldn't understand how their husbands found salvation elsewhere
Like in the deep shadows of her chocolate kissing thighs

Under red dresses

No wonder they all keep coming back.

They wanted to crawl between her parted legs and rest.

Make themselves at home.

Dragon Lady

I heard she got lungs built like honey combs
Built out of rubble
Legs like Chicago street lights
She steps into darkness with comfort
She builds homes in the slum of he-say-she-say

I heard someone called her a dragon once
Men gape at her like scales sit on her back
Women gape at her like
she is a creature who use to save
                                    nowadays
            Can only settle for being   a caged monster
                        Confined to the fears of *other*

In the beginning
Colored girls pose no threat
And only in secret
Can be kissed
Carried from whisper to whisper

The gossip left us sticky
With curiosity
With the mess all over our hands and mouths

We point and talk about her!
A side show bearded dragon lady!
What clowns our chatter made us into!
What an enigma our chatter made her into!

I heard someone called her a dragon once
Her confidence left Bones in amber
She could bend the amber of gossip and thoughts of the world to

ashes
Dance on them

She was a ritual people found scary
How someone could be
Untamable

Free

In love with herself
They didn't know
She knew
No lover
Amount of money
Amount of sex
Amount of liquor
Made her dance like the he-say-she-say slum

It is an Every. Day. Job.
To remember she is
Blameless
Soft
Esoteric

Battalions

of
Misogyny
Capitalism
Colorism
Sexism
Come dressed. Full body armor.
Such small minds to think that they could tame
A dragon
A mother

A guardian
A welcomer of fear
A truster of her own intuition
Corded with gold and wonder

I heard they talked about her nonstop
Couldn't stop even if they tried
She is everything she has ever needed
And always has been
"How?" they wonder
"How fascinating." They wonder
A woman. Brown. And curved. And admired. And warrior.
How (can) she be vulnerable and exposed and unafraid?

They couldn't do anything but see her

Despite their tries to revoke her right to be here

I see you.
I recognize you.

part IV. Lessons from mama and nem

"How simple a thing it seems to me that to know ourselves as we are, we must know our mother's names."

—Alice Walker

Visits with Dad

Have always made me uncomfortable
When I started to really get to know
my father
aloof
We would drive for an hour
From Indianapolis to Anderson
Where he lived with his new family
I thought on this hard

Thought about how much
I have missed out on for seven summers
Back home With my cousins

He seemed
Just as uncomfortable
"How is school,"
"...your mother"
"...your family"
"... (insert specific person he can no longer
Have a relationship with once ties were cut off with my
mother)."

Icebreaker
Old questions
And just as we arrived
I dreaded that blue house
To Anderson where he lived with his new family
                    The conversation seemed more fluid
                    We were pulling into the driveway

As I had entered a new world
Of children

And woman
(To learn of as mother)
Black woman

She valued
God, Family, Church
Home-cooked supper
Something father seeked from
Women based off his own mother,
I assumed

The weekend would pass and
We would be back in the car heading
Home to Indianapolis

The last time we drove to Anderson
Was right before
He was still married to his second wife

We rode home
uncomfortable
I was crying
I didn't understand
We made it to my mother's home

He had felt the same things she did
Years ago, she
Would go on to say
As she tells me she understands his pain.

adnaw

A drug addict taught me how to pray

She didn't know
she saved my life
When she
Split bible spines to show me
Life's compass inside
and to show me
how the human body is a cryptic coded telescope
to find God

"Close your eyes,
Clasp hands,
And bow your head,"
She said

Then she pointed
to a constellation
in my heart to
let me know
God was never missing

With Marlboro breath
and a knotted stomach
She showed me
the hard part about
having a relationship
with the spirit was letting go
Of who you use to be

or who you thought you were

She was a raped 5-year old
clawing at the insides
of a 36-year-old woman's body
begging to be loved or let go

With Marlboro breath and knotted stomach
She was worn out elastic
Like an old ponytail holder
No bounce back
Just crusted band
Scrunched between
Fears of losing her son again and
Fears of losing the high again

Hard to keep a job
Hard to keep a home
Hard to be keep a man

But not hard to keep praising
Not hard to keep feigning
Her praises
Random
Would dart into the air

Rip between the sheets of lonely
unzip a bag of blessings
With nowhere to put them
but back into the past
On days when she wished to be

Hooked

By the mouth or wrist to a line

But I've never known Jesus to fish by net.
To fill you all up at once.
As if he were filling up a room of 5,000 people. After
walking on water.
Scared as shit toward him.

She taught me about real faith
How being redeemed is dirtier than it sounds

She taught me
we don't know how beautiful we are
we turn our temples into tombstones
Stuck with fear

She taught me about the real revolution
is in loving yourself at your worst
the same way you love yourself at your best

She taught me pain
was the real drug that's hard to get away from

She taught me that she and I
are more alike than we are separate

So, I came to the meeting

Hello, my name is Chantel Massey
and I am an addict.

Black Sheep (mule of the world)

We have been
Both the audience
And the performer

Both the mess
And the masterpiece

Woman

Not a punching bag
Or quixotic sick fantasy

Instead we are queens
Erudite of many things
We create
We are ancient Kemet
Giving birth to kings and diamonds
With spirits that spring like March
And so we will fight for them
The way Israelites fought Pharaoh
We are Moses

We are the moment Nina Simone first touched a piano
We are Maya Angelou's first class in Ghana
We are Nikki Giovanni's "Ego Tripping"
Wine sipping

After a long day

Of being nectar and ambrosia

Woman is infinite

Woman is wisdom

We are the hopes of people bursting out of
Ferguson riots
Igniting confusion across continents

We are the hump in America's right eyebrow
Leaving them filled
With the curiosity of 1st grade classrooms
Asking how can *we* be
The first supernova

"It's simple,"
I tell them:
We are a myriad of generations
Dancing on the rings of Saturn
One century at a time

Stardust landing on mysterious planes
Sparking brains
And brightening hearts of
Your spirit's past life

We are made up of galaxies

We are the revolution

Clothed in defiance
Yet undefined
Bloody knuckles from
Shattering glass ceilings
And two-way mirrors

For

We not just any kind of woman

We *ain't* just any *kind of* woman

We are the kind in a bible and on the pole
Yet undefined

And that's ok

Because we,
we are made
in the image of God, *too*:

We are the fire cracker
lit the wrong way
On the fourth of July
So *oohh* and *aahh* at our
Bursting colors and flames
Cinders flying in
Unpredictable directions
Leaving old versions of self behind
Forever evolving

For

We are Love
We are life

We are both the mess and the masterpiece
I put that line in here twice for a reason
Every day as I learn what it means to be a woman
From my mother, my sisters, and all women around me

I learn
With faith like a mustard seed
There is nothing we cannot do

We are the eye of the hurricane
Even as we stand face to face with disaster,

We are still the destruction

We are black sheep.

Numb (or: 10 things you'd rather
find than missing black girls)

I bet you look for your phone when you can't find it
And your keys
And your remote control
And your hat
And your hair tie
And your sock
And your favorite shoes
And your car in the parking lot
When you come out of the store
You'd rather be late than not have that phone
I know you freak out
when you lose your keys
What about a child?
When you sit in the park
and can't find your kid
Imagine 34 black girls
Some for years
Some still in counting
But you better not lose your phone
In a park
At a store
On the subway
Or in an airport

Where was the last place you put your values?

Ode to Nina Simone

I'll take a crack at it, Liz

Maybe if Nina Simone
danced more after a glass of wine
She would have felt less lonely
Music can do that
Pussy stank and all

After a long
Work
day

there are

No worries about men
And what they find sexy

However, I hear they find
nothing sexier than confidence

Fear can make you

forget

about that type of freedom

like forgetting the place,
you put your keys,
but you know you brought
them with you.

Whose Roles Is Whose?

The breaking from Mama
started with a boy
12
the age I started to move from
her, question her

that has always been hard for her
saying that I am the only one

now I watch
as she begs for me
to fill a void she fooled herself
into believing I could fill since the beginning
never wanting this type of change
because it wasn't on her terms
My growth means I don't need her, she tells herself

the breaking from Mama wasn't easy
but necessary
unavoidable

painful to see we needed to be more
than mother and daughter for
one another
but so many times the roles got
confused
like whose roles is whose
that's all we could be
Like "Mama, it's ok." I'd tell her.
Face buried in her knees,
On kitchen floors
With a broken heart

Mature and nurturing for a
5 year old
7 year old
8 year old To
                    A 28 year old
                        30 year old
                        31 year old

Hard to know
Who belonged where
Emotions vs bills
I guess made things tricky

Sometimes
She would stay with Aunt
I believed it was for her to
Figure out those roles
Places
Of woman
Of Black
Of Mother

I would inquire about her own mother,
This woman who I mirror in nose, mouth, and eyes
This woman who would have loved me
Had she known me longer,
Than a year
They say,
This woman who did not have
The best relationship with Mama

They tell me, *my* aunts,
Mama was angry with her

For not being there
For giving so much of herself
To her 6 *other* children
GrandMama fell ill and
Unavailable
Left Mama exposed and
Longing for mother
But found it in three other sisters

They,
    too,
        all got their roles confused

Some would later confess
Others would deny
And say that's why
Things can't be different

They never fixed the roles

Didn't know when to be a sister vs how to be a mother

And often left the woman,
The dreamer,
The free spirit
The wanderer in Mama
Also longing for a blueprint of her own mother

I like to think I understand her more now that I am older

Because shit I have been
Longing for a blueprint of *my* mother too.

part V. The making of half a woman

"I worked hard to love me and become the woman I am."

—Carmen Guess

Half-Ass

"You must unlearn your mother's ways to learn love," I remind
myself.
To finish. To learn self.
To get out of your own way.
I must unlearn:
Safety
The half loving
The half doing

My mother
has never been one
To finish
So what else do I know other than
To meet my lover half way
And even that's hard
Because lover will see how, some days,
I feel like I am half the moon,
Like my mother
Taking up part of the night

Lover will learn my obsession with completion
"You must finish." I remind myself

And then I remember my mother
How she cooked half a meal
She painted half the house
She traveled only half the world
Because she gave all her heart to half a man

She did things like that
My mother: half doing
My mother be the half making

Making a daughter into half a woman
And leaving the rest for her to do

A tongue that is half-dirty and half-holy
Covered in half-French, half-English
And tells half the truth half the time
To protect me
To protect daughter
To protect half a woman
Who fed off half her chest
But not afraid to give her whole heart
But afraid for me to find out about this world and how it
could make
An empty space out of me
Just blank black body
And a number
A hashtag

I see how she half did
She had half the faith
Because for her whole life
She had to be a whole woman
Who had half the love
Half the history
And half created the rest
For legacy to give to her Chantel,
her child
Wild seed
Wall flower
Watching mama
Get dressed
Go to work
Love me
Love some man who don't deserve her.

24

The older I get the more I learn to surrender
With my grandmother's hips and my mother's eyes
I can milk you a glass of moons and
honeycomb you a sea of stars of all the times
I've been set on fire like a hungover sunray

I wear mama's "you will understand,"
around my neck
like diamonds now
Oh how
I've learned
it's not enough
to be holy and wild and tangled
like coils caught in plastic teeth

Peel open my chest
and you'll find a pulse heavy and pursed
with tangy redemptions from too many nights
where my mind would furl any fear into a forbidden lake

Whether it be the hope that the cross I bare
don't just up and look like a target one day
Or the fear that loneliness will know my name all too well
Skinny dip and be all the vulnerable
I never give myself permission to be during the day
With depression button, down my back

Coconut knees on skinny long copper legs
I step into yesterday so many times
I forget how to be here

How to bask in my grandfather's amazement that this is all
my hair

I thank god that he is beautiful and 74 as he leans in his
recliner

The older I get I must remember to laugh
I let laughter juggle around in my belly
like loose change in my pocketbook
to put my fears in place
To not fold into myself like burning paper

Remember to be encouraged

Remember, I am a walking history of women
who rose like a phoenix from the ashes in this noisy world

This spirit
Lit, like a 1963 Buddhist protestor again and again

Pious and crimson
I tell their story of being black
and woman
and miscarriages
and journeys to meet god, lost children, gossip, rape,
cancer
and being broken
and rising
and rising
and rising

The older I get
the more I know crosses are as red as targets
Feel the same in weight

Sound the same when they hit the ground
The same way bodies sway in trees look
like ones caught in the reel of the wind
after a bullet passes through the chest

I know legal is not synonymous with right
I know prayers to God sound like a frayed candle wick whispered
cry after it's burn started to spread and still be heard

I know seasons will change
I know I will leave the same way I came:
Alone
I know my crown might be heavy, but it ain't coming off
The older I get the more I know my anger is just sadness
I know I am messed up
I also know I am blessed
The older I get the more I know my mama was right

The older I get the more I learn to surrender
With my grandmother's hips and my mother's eyes
I can milk you a glass of moons and
honey comb you a sea of stars of all the times
I've been set on fire like a hungover sunray

I wear mama's "you will understand," around my neck like
diamonds now.

My personified loneliness, Bones I

I would open my home to you but
It isn't clean
A heavy body bag
Sits under the bed
of my heart
Molding
Hands beside hips
Dirt under fingernails
Chin lying to chest
Leaving a smell
I haven't quite made out what
Type of smell
It's different
Like the first time I masturbated
Sinful but refreshing

I haven't removed it yet

Its spirit roams this house
Moaning and speaking
Existing in my space

Loneliness was once a real person
He lived in this house
He was deceased
After going to war with forgiveness
Over my broken heart

Arguing about who should be the one
To move in and clean up
To heal
But Loneliness didn't come to clean

It was just looking for a host
Now its spirit walks around with black eyes and a hollow
form

We met in a bed of alcohol
We frolicked between sheets of vodka bottle like insomniacs
together

He convinced me he could cure me

Revive forgotten feelings
He could make me feel like
I was living again

But at the expense of my dignity and frugality
I had to understand
It would be ephemeral

But if I wanted more
I would have to keep coming back

Because misery loves company.

Bones II

I dread the Loneliness
How it festers
In the back of my mind
And in the brittle of my bones
Even when I stand
In the wave of a crowd
It boils me to a smoke
Filling me for a moment
As I try to
Run away from it
Over and over again

I was born into it
So, if I am socially awkward
Or turn into a phantom
Know this is why.

American dream after the mourning of July 5th, 2016

Days like today
leaves start to collect in the gutter
I sit and ignore it
I read.
Dogs bark.
It rains for a while
I think.
CNN drops another story:
black male. neck pressed
forearms and elbows left
body suffocated like a dried raisin

Bullets secure the kill
lungs now
a glass bowl
Hitting the ground

Hunting season is year-round
a pebble hits the pond
the grief spreads
for mother
                son
                    daughter
                        niece
                            nephew
                    brother
                sister
        friend

"37-year-old Alton Sterling shot and
killed by Baton Rouge officer Tuesday morning."

Mourning knew no love like a bullet to a black body

-plays clip of grieving family-
The sensation of watching
Black families mourn
Be torn apart

Isn't new
By failure to signal or failure to remain quiet and just comply
It's hard to believe they don't like us like this
"officers say they thought he had a gun."
-news plays video-
"He has a gun," Officer shouted
-gun shot-
-gun shot-
-gun shot-
person recording screams
-cut back to reporter-
"It has been reported that officers will go on administrative leave."
I hear the rain beat the gutters,
The pain boils over
The anger I feel from the desensitized conversations,
The: "Well did he have a gun? Why was he selling CDs out there? Just take this as a lesson."
"If you speak to a police officer remember to be respectful."
"Be careful not to be aggressive."
As if my existence isn't threat enough
Mama torn between I-want-you-to-live-so-hush-and-do-what-they-say
Vs.
You-deserve-to-live-on-the-edge-naturally

Because being followed by the police is a constant cliff hanger
Lesson from *black* survival guide 101:
Watch out for the landmines
"Officer, I don't understand what I am being searched for."
-gun shot-
"Officer I am just reaching for my information."
-gun shot-
"Officer, could you just tell me what I did wrong?"
-gun shot-
Curl yourself into a chameleon
Code switch
your tongue.
Twist your mouth into a strange fruit circus side show
into

A.

W.E.B. DuBois Double Consciousness experiment
So that they don't see color
And hope it works
like laws that protect the officers

B.

Cause: there is not enough evidence to warrant charges
against officers from videos or witnesses
Days like today
leaves start to collect in the gutter
I notice how the house feels different
Curtains closed
I watch the TV
I notice how they fight for this gorilla
Value is the question

Where does it lie?
Who determines it?
I notice how they fight for this gorilla
But not Alton Sterling
Not Tamir Rice
Not Sandra Bland
-cut from graphic video of gorilla
back to your regularly scheduled programing—

"When we return, we will talk about this new grill coming
out.
And what really happened on the east side in last night's
shooting."

-cut to commercial-

Dogs bark, again
I remember
I am a stranger, here, in this home
On this land
I remember
On my way, inside
I walked past the white picket fence
Close it behind me
Walked past the dogs
For they did not recognize
The same one who built the house
Two stories
Red door
White home
Blue shutters
Green yard
I came for my forty acres and my mule
Inside this home

53

I stand here with the plan of dismantlement
A woman,
Silent and dis\\ruptive
This home
This dream just met its nightmare.

Some Days

Sometimes
even on Sunday
I am Jacob returning to Bethel as Isaac
God will find me the same way God left me
A child of Hers
Full and joyful
Playing with ruins and ruble of the past
Rebuilding the way, I was told

Learning that being defeated
Or having my ribs broken
Are just battle wounds

Learning that losing in a cave
Designed to make me a maven
Is where I meet the river
And die to be resurrected
Allow my body to be
Carried off into the stream
Facing the heavens

Some days I am Joseph
Some days I am David

Other days I am barely
Keeping it together

Some days I am yearning

Other days I am just a woman

still learning

Just a woman

Who still knows

that the only thing I know

is nothing.

references

The constellations of quotations bursting through this book were discovered at For Harriet, an online community for women of African ancestry. Discover more at:

web
http://www.forharriet.com/2012/03/85-quotes-from-black-women-to-inspire.html#ixzz4lMesYwbZ

Twitter
@ForHarriet

Facebook
forharriet

about the author

Multifaceted artist, actress, and educator, Chantel Massey is most commonly known for her poetry writing and riveting performances. After receiving her Bachelor's degree in English from the College of Wooster, where she co-started the campus poetry club with Lee McKinstry, Chantel went on to teach in inner-city schools in Indianapolis and continued to write and perform.

An Indianapolis native, Chantel has performed across various local platforms. In 2015, Massey played as Dorothy in *Wizar of Odd* written by dynamic poet Gabrielle Patterson as a poetry rendition of *The Wizard of Oz*. In 2016, she worked for Act Out, an IUPUI social justice acting organization, that trained organizations in diversity inclusion and social justice.

Chantel has opened for Co-founding member of Black Lives Matter Movement, Elle Hearns, two-time National Poetry Slam Champion, Anis Mojgani, and has spoken, performed, hosted, and led workshops for organizations, schools, and programs. Currently she teaches at an all-girls middle school, where she encourages students to independently critique ideas, self-advocate, work hard, and be resilient.

Chantel is authentic and original in her writing and performances. She facilitates spaces for her audience and reader to experience the words for themselves. As a passionate writer and poet who loves to play with imagery exploring human rights, womanhood, sexuality, religion, spirituality, and more, Chantel wishes to inspire others through art to think better and higher about themselves and each other through self-expression. Chantel is passionate about education, youth development, art and self-expression. She finds inspiration from the women in her family, Nikki Giovanni, Toni Morrison, Joshua Bennett, Nina Simone, Maya Angelou, Miles Hodges, Jasmine Mans, and Alicia

Made in the USA
Lexington, KY
15 April 2018